Liv[...]
Y[...]
the[...]
Enjoy every step
along the way. Life is
short - relax and enjoy
the adventure!

Love Janet
2006

As you begin to pay attention to your own

stories and what they say about you, you

will enter into the exciting process of becoming,

as you should be, the author of your own

life, the creator of your own possibilities.

MANDY AFTEL

ACKNOWLEDGEMENTS

WITH SPECIAL THANKS TO

Jason Aldrich, Gerry Baird, Jay Baird, Neil Beaton, Doug Cruickshank, Jim Darragh, Jennifer & Matt Ellison, Josie & Rob Estes, Michael Flynn, Jennifer Hurwitz, Liam Lavery, Connie McMartin, Cristal & Brad Olberg, Janet Potter & Family, Aimee Rawlins, Diane Roger, Drew Wilkie, Robert & Mary Anne Wilkie, Heidi & Shale Yamada, Justi, Tote & Caden Yamada, Robert & Val Yamada, Kaz, Kristin, Kyle & Kendyl Yamada, Tai & Joy Yamada, Anne Zadra, August & Arline Zadra and Dan Zadra.

CREDITS

Compiled by Kobi Yamada
Designed by Steve Potter

ACHIEVE every day.

COMPENDIUM™
PUBLISHING

live inspired.

Your future depends
on many things,
but mostly on you.

FRANK TYGER

People are capable,
at any time in their
lives, of doing what
they dream of.

BETH BINGHAM

ACHIEVE every day.

What we focus
on increases.

ROB ESTES

We write our
own destiny.
We become
what we do.

MADAME CHIANG KAI-SHEK

The future was
plump with
promise.

MAYA ANGELOU

Each day comes to
me with both hands
full of possibilities.

HELEN KELLER

ACHIEVE every day.

Whether or not
you reach your
goals in life
depends entirely
on how well you
prepare for them
and how badly
you want them.

RONALD MCNAIR

I set my star so
high that I would
constantly be in
motion towards it.

SIDNEY POITIER

You must begin
to think of yourself
as becoming the
person you want
to be.

STEPHEN VIZINCZEY

People become
who they are.
Even Beethoven
became Beethoven.

ACHIEVE every day.

Give something
a name, and
it will happen.

BOB BOWEN

ACHIEVE every day.

Everything big
starts little.

UNKNOWN

You create your
opportunities by
asking for them.

PATTY HANSEN

To find an open
road, have an
open mind.

JOHN TOWNE

ACHIEVE every day.

Make your goal
tangible by sharing
it with others.
Say it out loud
and put it on
paper. Often.

RHONDA ABRAMS

Never run out
of goals.

EARL NIGHTINGALE

Find a purpose in
life so big it will
challenge every
capacity to be at
your best.

JIM LOEHR

When two paths
open before you,
take the harder one.

What you do today
can improve all
your tomorrows.

RALPH MARSTON

When you put
yourself whole-
heartedly into
something, energy
grows. It seems
inexhaustible.

HELEN DE ROSIS

There is more in
us than we know.
If we can be made
to see it, perhaps,
for the rest of our
lives, we will be
unwilling to settle
for less.

KURT HAHN

ACHIEVE every day.

You can achieve
anything you want
in life if you have
the courage to
dream it, the
intelligence to
make a realistic
plan, and the will
to see that plan
through to the end.

SIDNEY A. FRIEDMAN

ACHIEVE every day.

You are not made
for failure, you are
made for victory.
Go forward with
joyful confidence.

GEORGE ELIOT

ACHIEVE every day.

It's not a matter of
'if' but a matter of
'when.'

JIM DANIELL

ACHIEVE every day.

The faster you
learn, the bigger
you win.

JIM HAUDAN

Big results
require big
ambitions.

JAMES CHAMPY

When we strive to become better than we are, everything around us becomes better, too.

KOBI YAMADA

So what do we
do? Anything.
Something. So long
as we just don't sit
there. If we screw
it up, start over.
Try something else.
If we wait until
we've satisfied all
the uncertainties,
it may be too late.

LEE IACOCCA

We must walk
consciously only
part way toward
our goal, and then
leap in the dark
to our success.

HENRY DAVID THOREAU

ACHIEVE every day.

Dreams in life may
seem impossible.
They are not.
Impossible dreams
are achieved one
goal at a time.   .

HERMAN CAIN

There can be
no success or
happiness if the
things we believe
in are different
from the things
we do.

FREYA MADELINE STARK

The first requisite
for success is the
ability to apply
your physical and
mental energies
to one problem
incessantly without
growing weary.

THOMAS EDISON

ACHIEVE every day.

I wasn't afraid to
fail. Something
good always comes
out of failure.

ANNE BAXTER

Nothing's far
when one wants
to get there.

QUEEN MARIE OF RUMANIA

Enthusiasm is the
great hill-climber.

ELBERT HUBBARD

ACHIEVE every day.

Spectacular
achievements are
always preceded
by unspectacular
preparation.

ROGER STAUBACH

The will to win
is worthless if you
do not have the
will to prepare.

THANE YOST

Every worthwhile
accomplishment,
big or little, has its
stages of drudgery
and triumph:
a beginning,
a struggle, and
a victory.

MAHATMA GANDHI

ACHIEVE every day.

The only way
to excellence is
to consistently
improve yourself
every single day.

THOMAS J. VILORD

ACHIEVE every day.

Just when you
think you know
exactly how it's
going, some other
possibility shows
up and it gets
even better.

NILS EKSTROM

ACHIEVE every day.

Either you reach a
higher point today,
or you exercise
your strength in
order to be able
to climb higher
tomorrow.

FRIEDRICH NIETZSCHE

ACHIEVE every day.

You can do what
you want to do;
sometimes you can
do it even better
than you thought
you could.

JIMMY CARTER

Don't let anything
stop you. There
will be times when
you'll be disap-
pointed, but you
can't stop. Make
yourself the very
best that you can
make of what you
are. The very best.

SADIE T. ALEXANDER

ACHIEVE every day.

Ask yourself,
"How long am I
going to work to
make my dreams
come true?"
I suggest you
answer, "As long
as it takes."

JIM ROHN

There is freedom
in stepping out
and taking risks
when you know at
any given moment,
you can always
begin again.

EVA GREGORY

ACHIEVE every day.

There is no such
thing as failure;
there is only
success or quitting.
I'm not a quitter.

UNKNOWN

Every strike brings
me closer to the
next home run.

BABE RUTH

The potential of
the average person
is like a huge ocean
unsailed, a new
continent unexplored,
a world of possibilities
waiting to be released
and channeled toward
some great good.

BRIAN TRACY

If your instinct is
to wait, ponder
and perfect, then
you're dead.

RUTHANN QUINDLEN

We must stop
assuming that a
thing which has
never been done
before probably
cannot be done
at all.

DONALD M. NELSON

Almost all really
new ideas have a
certain aspect of
foolishness when
they are first
produced.

ALFRED N. WHITEHEAD

I don't believe in
failure. It is not
failure if you
enjoyed the process.

OPRAH WINFREY

ACHIEVE every day.

Learning too soon
our limitations,
we never learn
our powers.

MIGNON MCLAUGHLIN

ACHIEVE every day.

The problems of the world cannot possibly be solved by skeptics or cynics whose horizons are limited by the obvious realities. We need men and women who can dream of things that never were.

JOHN F. KENNEDY

ACHIEVE every day.

The way I see it,
there are two kinds
of dreams. One
is a dream that's
always going to
be just that...
a dream. Then
there's a dream
that's more than
a dream; it's like...
a map.

ROBERT COOPER

Learn to say "no"
to the good, so
you can say "yes"
to the great.

JOHN MASON

You've achieved
success in your
field when you
don't know whether
what you're doing
is work or play.

WARREN BEATTY

A day you waste is
one you can never
make up.

GEORGE ALLEN

It is better to be
prepared for an
opportunity and
not have one
than to have an
opportunity and
not be prepared.

WHITNEY YOUNG, JR.

ACHIEVE every day.

If we are to
achieve results
never before
accomplished,
we must expect
to employ methods
never before
attempted.

FRANCIS BACON

ACHIEVE every day.

No matter what
the level of your
ability, you have
more potential
than you can ever
develop in a
lifetime.

JAMES T. MCCAY

Stop thinking
about what you
can achieve; think
about what you
can contribute...
This is how you
will achieve.

PETER DRUCKER

ACHIEVE every day.

Success is not
counted by how
high you have
climbed but by
how many you have
brought with you.

WIL ROSE

Surround yourself
with people who
are only going to
lift you higher.

OPRAH WINFREY

All that you
accomplish or fail
to accomplish with
your life is the
direct result of
your thoughts.

JAMES ALLEN

ACHIEVE every day.

It is not enough to
aim, you must hit.

ITALIAN PROVERB

In a pond koi can reach lengths of eighteen inches. Amazingly, when placed in a lake, koi can grow to three feet long. The metaphor is obvious. You are limited by how you see the world.

VINCE POSCENTE

I learned that
there were two
ways I could live
my life: following
my dreams or
doing something
else. Dreams aren't
a matter of chance,
but a matter of
choice. When I
dream, I believe
I am rehearsing
my future.

DAVID COPPERFIELD

ACHIEVE every day.

Leaders don't
wait. They shape
their own frontiers.
The bigger the
challenge, the greater
the opportunity.

UNKNOWN

ACHIEVE every day.

Patience,
persistence and
perspiration make
an unbeatable
combination for
success.

NAPOLEAN HILL

ACHIEVE every day.

Success is peace
of mind, which
is a direct result
of knowing you
did your best to
become the best
that you are capable
of becoming.

JOHN WOODEN

The only way to
enjoy anything in
this life is to earn
it first.

GINGER ROGERS

ACHIEVE every day.

It had long since
come to my attention
that people of
accomplishment
rarely sat back
and let things
happen to them.
They went out and
happened to things.

ELINOR SMITH

ACHIEVE every day.

Business is
optimism.

CHAD MACKAY

Possibilities do
not add up. They
multiply.

PAUL M. ROMER

Failures, repeated
failures, are finger
posts on the road
to achievement.
One fails forward
toward success.

CHARLES KETTERING

Don't just do it,
do it well.

KARI CASSIDY

Declare your
mission and
then live it!

TOM WELCH

A true measure of
your worth includes
all the benefits
others have gained
from your success.

CULLEN HIGHTOWER

ACHIEVE every day.

Remember,
nobody wins unless
everybody wins.

BRUCE SPRINGSTEEN

Dream with your
eyes open.

ERNST HAAS

Never turn down
an opportunity
because you think
it's too small;
you don't know
where it can lead.

JULIA MORGAN

Those who choose
the beginning of a
road, also choose
its destination.

ANONYMOUS

ACHIEVE every day.

If today will not,
tomorrow may.

THOMAS FULLER

Perhaps this
very instant is
your time.

LOUISE BOGAN

ACHIEVE every day.

Save the world
around you from
unfulfilled
potential.

UNKNOWN

To dream anything
that you want to
dream. That's
the beauty of the
human mind. To
do anything that
you want to do.
That is the strength
of the human spirit.

BERNARD EDMONDS

The difference
between a
calculated risk
and rolling the
dice can be
expressed in one
word: homework.

GEORGETTE MOSEBACHER

ACHIEVE every day.

Go back a little
to leap the further.

FRENCH PROVERB

ACHIEVE every day.

The line between
failure and success
is so fine that we
scarcely know when
we pass it: So fine
that we are often on
the line and do not
even know it.

ELBERT HUBBARD

ACHIEVE every day.

Success never rests. On your worst days, be good. And on your best days, be great. And on every other day, get better.

CARMEN MARIANO

Limited expectations
yield only limited
results.

SUSAN LAURSON WILLIG

ACHIEVE every day.

The only limit to
our realization of
tomorrow will be our
doubts of today. Let
us move forward with
strong and active faith.

FRANKLIN D. ROOSEVELT

An idea isn't
worth much until
the person is found
who has the energy
and ability to make
it work.

WILLIAM FEATHER

Whatever I focus
on in my mind,
expands. My mind
is a powerful tool
I have for creating
the life I want.

JODY STEVENSON

You can't
reach a goal
you haven't set.

RHONDA ABRAMS

Destiny is not a
matter of chance,
it is a matter of
choice; it is not
a thing to be
waited for, it is a
thing to be achieved.

WILLIAM JENNINGS BRYAN

Boldness, more
boldness, and
always boldness!

GEORGE JACQUES DANTON

ACHIEVE every day.

It shall be done
sometime,
somewhere.

OPHELIA GUYON BROWNING

ACHIEVE every day.

Be careful what
you think and
say. Life might be
listening and give
you less next time.

KOBI YAMADA

ACHIEVE every day.

Commitment is
critical for
making changes.
Let's make our
deadlines and
due dates mean
something.

RHONDA ABRAMS

ACHIEVE every day.

Everyone must
row with the
oars he has.

ENGLISH PROVERB

ACHIEVE every day.

When we dim
our light, we
invite mediocrity.

KRIS KING

He who wishes to secure the good of others has already secured his own.

CONFUCIUS

The ability to
form friendships,
to make people
believe in you
and trust you,
is one of the
few absolutely
fundamental
qualities of
success.

JOHN J. MCGUIRK

.You are today
where your
thoughts have
brought you;
you will be
tomorrow where
your thoughts
take you.

JAMES ALLEN

You are a living
magnet. What you
attract into your
life is in harmony
with your dominant
thoughts.

BRIAN TRACY

The dream is not up
there in the sky or
the stars. It's right
here in your heart.

DAN ZADRA

Actions are the
seeds of fate;
deeds grow
into destiny.

A.L. LINALL

ACHIEVE every day.

Be a Columbus
to whole new
continents and
worlds within you,
opening new
channels, not of
trade, but of thought.

HENRY DAVID THOREAU

ACHIEVE every day.